All Creatures Pour Out Speech

TESTIMONIES OF WISDOM

by

NEAL A. BRINGE, Ph.D.

Creation Speech

Least Chipmunk at home at 12,000 feet, James Peak Wilderness, Colorado, September 17, 2018

Published by CreationSpeech
CreationSpeech.com

ISBN: 978-0-9984154-7-5

Library of Congress Control Number: 2019901243

Printed in the United States of America.

Testimonies of Wisdom: *"O Lord, how manifold are your works! In wisdom have you made them all; the earth is full of your creatures."* (Psalm 104:24)

FRONT COVER PHOTO: The broad-tailed hummingbird and the hollyhock flowers were made with wisdom to supply food for the bird, pollination for the flower and a teaching moment to a child about the glory of God.

TO THE PRAISE OF THE
multi-splendor of God's wisdom
AND THE glory of His grace

Contents

Introduction

KNOW GOD

God is Mighty

God is Good & Merciful

Live in the Spirit & Do Good Works for God

Tell Others About God

Submit to God

ACKNOWLEDGEMENTS

I am grateful to the Holy Spirit for inspiring me in the Lord Jesus Christ to glorify God with the contents of this book. Joshua & Jessica Schwisow and Sarah Bryant were a gift in laying out the book so it is attractive and professional. Becky Morecraft, Dalton Lockman and Pastor Kevin Swanson were gracious to proofread the text. My wife Lida was a great support in sharing the adventure of exploring God's creation with our children.

Seagulls, North Shore of Lake Superior, August 24, 2006

How can we help the next generation know God and walk humbly with Him?

God's Word: In Scripture, God reveals who He is and how we are to walk with Him. His Word is perfect, reviving the soul; sure, making wise the simple; right, rejoicing the heart; pure, enlightening the eyes; clean, true, and righteous altogether (Psalm 19:7-11).

God's Creation: God reveals the truth of His Word through His creation. Day to day, God's creation pours out speech and knowledge that is found in His Word.

"The heavens declare the glory of God,
and the sky above proclaims his handiwork.
Day to day pours out speech, and night to night reveals knowledge....
The testimony of the Lord is sure, making wise the simple."
(PSALM 19:1-3,7)

We can help the next generation grasp Scripture by showing it illustrated in God's creation. For example, seagulls flying and calling, roaring waves, and colorful rocks and plants of the coastlands are a testimony of God's reign:

"The LORD reigns, let the earth rejoice,
let the many coastlands be glad."
(PSALM 97:1)

Apply the metaphor of the coastlands. Rejoice in the LORD's reign by *"singing psalms and hymns and spiritual songs with thankfulness in your hearts to God"* (Colossians 3:16).

Along the way in this book, I provided sample prayers to encourage praise to God as you read. Take these words and add your own as you and your family give praise and adoration to the Creator. Consider reading 1-2 pages of the book a day as a devotional and meditate on the greatness of God.

"On your wondrous works, I will meditate"

Lesser Goldfinches, Elizabeth, Colorado, August 31, 2018

God's works speak the truth of His Word. His numerous creatures tell of His splendor, majesty, greatness, and goodness.

"On the glorious splendor of your majesty, and on your wondrous works, I will meditate. They shall speak of the might of your awesome deeds, and I will declare your greatness. They shall pour forth the fame of your abundant goodness and shall sing aloud of your righteousness."
(PSALM 145:5-7)

Everything that was made is significant, even flowers, butterflies, turtles and birds. God used the picture of birthing mountain goats, the freedom of wild donkeys, the strength of horses, and the migration of hawks, to illustrate who He was to Job (Job 39). The pictures helped Job to understand His position before God.

"I had heard of you by the hearing of the ear, but now my eye sees you; therefore I despise myself, and repent in dust and ashes."
(JOB 42:5-6)

Flame Skimmer Dragonfly, Boiling River, Yellowstone National Park, Wyoming, July 29, 2018

KNOW GOD

God is Mighty

I sing the mighty power of God
That made the mountains rise,
That spread the flowing seas
Abroad and built the lofty skies.
I sing the wisdom that ordained
The sun to rule the day;
The moon shines full at His command,
And all the stars obey.

—*I Sing The Mighty Power of God*, Isaac Watts, 1715

Indian Paintbrush and Flea Beetle were created to have matching orange and purple colors, Elizabeth, Colorado, May 7, 2018

"The LORD is the everlasting God, the Creator of the ends of the earth. He does not faint or grow weary; his understanding is unsearchable."

(ISAIAH 40:28)

Broad-Tailed Hummingbird gathering nectar from Hollyhock flowers, Elizabeth, Colorado, July 21, 2018

God made trees, flowering plants (third day of creation) and birds (fifth day, Genesis 1) with the breath of His Word (Psalm 33:6). We cannot understand how that creative act is possible. Nor can we understand how God could know from the beginning how all the created parts would work together and depend on each other. For example, hummingbird tongues were made with flower structure and nectar in mind. When the special tongue of hummingbirds contact nectar, two tubes of the structure split and flaps unfurl and then reclose to trap the nectar as the tongue is withdrawn, all within a fraction of a second. At the same time, it was considered that the bird would enable pollen to be distributed so that plants could produce seeds. We can trust the commands of such an infinite God. Unlike us, He considers all things without growing weary.

"But ask the beasts, and they will teach you; the birds of the heavens, and they will tell you; ... and the fish of the sea will declare to you. Who among all these does not know that the hand of the LORD has done this? In his hand is the life of every living thing and the breath of all mankind." (JOB 12:7-10)

Young female Broad-Tailed Hummingbird, Elizabeth, Colorado, September 7, 2018

How do we know that God holds us in His hands, including every breath? An indirect way is by observing His creation of birds. We find that the birds are adorned with remarkable beauty, abilities, and protection, according to God's care.

Dear God, Thank you for giving us hope as we see your hand upholds all life.

"So God created the great sea creatures and every living creature that moves, with which the waters swarm, according to their kinds, and every winged bird according to its kind. And God saw that it was good."
(GENESIS 1:21)

Wild Turkeys, Parker, Colorado, March 24, 2015

Based on the truth of God's Word, we can classify different kinds of birds according to kinds. Pheasants, partridge, grouse, quail, chickens, and turkeys appear to be variations of one kind of bird, and hummingbirds are variations of another kind. Turkeys are incredible. It is amazing to see a 20-pound wild turkey run up to 30 miles per hour across a field. Alertness and good eye sight helps them survive among coyotes. They eat leaves, grasses, seeds, fruits, berries and (invasive) stink bugs. The males grunt, gobble, and strut about shaking their 25,000 feathers. Their wattle becomes bright red during the spring mating season.

Dear God, Thank you making the ground-loving fowl, including the turkey. Your mighty power is clearly seen in the use of your infinite creativity and wisdom to make whatsoever you please for your glory.

"Out of Zion, the perfection of beauty, God shines forth."
(PSALM 50:2)

God is the source of beauty. We can see it in His creation. My wife and I saw vividly colored macaws fly together in pairs over rain forests in Costa Rica. The colors of bird feathers can be formed by different means. Pigments in the feathers absorb certain wavelengths of light and structures in the feathers reflect certain wavelengths. Green colors of some parrots are the result of both yellow pigments and reflected blue light.

God's creation of beauty is ultimate in Zion, His city, His people, His kingdom.

Dear God, we pray "Your kingdom come, your will be done, on earth as it is in heaven" (Matthew 6:10).

Macaw, Wildlife World, Litchfield Park, Arizona, December 28, 2013

"Thus says the LORD, your Redeemer, who formed you from the womb: I am the Lord, who made all things, who alone stretched out the heavens, <u>who spread out the earth</u> by myself." (ISAIAH 44:24)

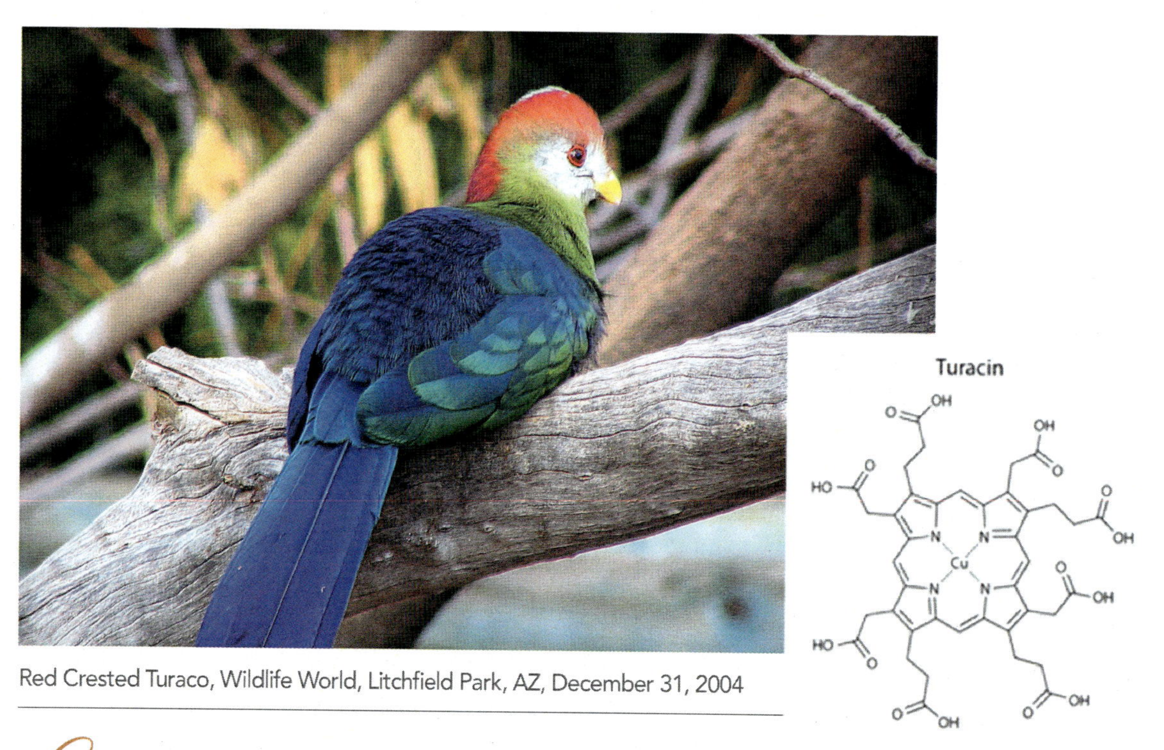

Red Crested Turaco, Wildlife World, Litchfield Park, AZ, December 31, 2004

God knew the environments that would exist on earth before He spread it out. With this foreknowledge He made birds able to live in each particular place so that they do not have to compete with all birds. For example, the Turaco birds were created with unique pigments that enable them to live in copper-rich areas of Africa. The bright red color of Turaco's crown is from complexes between uroporphyrin III and copper, called turacin, which fluoresce in ultraviolet light. Turacin reportedly is a break-down product of hemoglobin in the liver which combines with copper, collects in certain feathers and forms microcrystals (Blumberg, 1965). The pigments limit the birds exposure to dietary copper (fruits, seeds, leaves, flowers). So Turacos live in the copper-rich areas of Africa south of the Sahara from Angola, where they are the national bird, to the Congo. Other birds derive their red coloration from carotenoid or phaeomelanin pigments.

"And God blessed them, saying 'Be fruitful and multiply and fill the waters in the seas, and let the birds multiply on the earth.'" (GENESIS 1:22)

Steller's Jay, Sedalia Colorado, September 14, 2017

Canada Jay, Winter Park, CO, September 19, 2017

Steller's, Canada, and Blue Jays live in different environments as planned by God to multiply this bird kind around the earth. Perhaps only one representative was needed on Noah's ark during the worldwide flood. After the flood, a greater diversity of environments on earth may have triggered genetic responses that resulted in variations. So the birds multiplied on earth, filling the earth with God's glory. The feathers of the Stellar Jay consist of a matrix of keratin and air cells precisely structured to reflect blue light and allow other colors to be absorbed by a black melanin layer. We should be grateful to God for His attention to brighten our days with this beautiful bird! *"Praise the Lord . . . flying birds . . . Let them praise the name of the Lord, for his name alone is exalted; his majesty is above earth and heaven"* (Psalm 148:1a,10b,13).

"The mountains rose, the valleys sank down to the place that you appointed for them. You make springs gush forth in the valleys … they give drink to every beast of the field … Beside them the birds of the heavens dwell; they sing among the branches." (PSALM 104:8-12)

Meadowlark singing while horses graze on a distant hillside, Elizabeth, Colorado, May 29, 2017

In the springtime, I enjoyed listening to a western meadowlark singing, and watched horses grazing in the distance, with snow-covered Rocky Mountains beyond them. The scene is a reminder of Psalm 104:8-12. God made the mountains rise (verse 8). He provides water for the beasts of the field (verse 11). He made birds that perch on trees to sing (verse 12). Scripture is a trustworthy record the mighty power of God in history.

"But according to his promise we are waiting for new heavens and a new earth, in which righteousness dwells." (2 PETER 3:13)

Fossilized fish (Knightia, related to Herring), and feces were found after splitting open a slab of oil shale near Kemmerer, Wyoming (Green River Formation), August 4, 2004

God judged the earth which was filled with the violence of all flesh, by bringing about the worldwide flood. Fossils appear to be reminders of God's global judgement. The burial of creatures was so quick that even fish feces were fossilized. The Almighty God will once again judge the world when Jesus Christ returns. So the Apostle Peter wrote that *"we ought to be in lives of holiness and godliness ... waiting for new heavens and a new earth in which righteousness dwells"* (2 Peter 3:11b, 13).

"Blessed be the Lord God of Israel, for he has visited and redeemed his people and has raised up a horn of salvation for us." (LUKE 1:68-69A)

Big horn sheep, Glenwood Springs, Colorado, January 23, 2018

The powerful horned-heads of rams, cattle, and bison are a reminder of the power of God to save His people. As promised, He redeemed them from the Midianites and the Philistines. These works foreshadowed the death and resurrection of Jesus, who redeems all who believe this truth. Jesus is our horn of salvation. In Him we live for God and have victory over sin and death, by God's grace.

"This God is my strong refuge and has made my way blameless. He made my feet like the feet of a deer and set me secure on the heights." (2 SAMUEL 22:33-34)

"God, the Lord, is my strength; he makes my feet like the deer's; he makes me tread on my high places." (HABAKKUK 3:19)

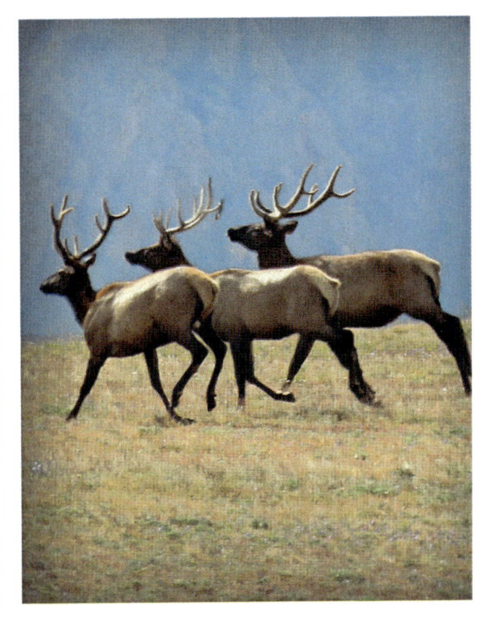

Bull Elk on Ridge above Deep Lake, Beartooth Plateau, WY, August 15, 2017

The deer kind includes moose, elk, red deer, white tail deer, and reindeer. The elks' strength enables them to trot gracefully through the mountains. They are a picture of our spiritual strength in the Lord. According to God's grace, we tread on the spiritual heights in victory over our enemies (the world, the flesh, the devil). The truth of His Word sets us free to live for the God of our salvation with sure and stable footing. As we abide in Jesus through prayer, patience, and hope, He enables us to travel through the valleys and hills of life with thanksgiving and expectation of victory in His power.

Dear God, thank you for helping us to see the strength that we have in you through faith in Jesus. You are the source of our strength and hope.

"Sanctify them in the truth; your word is truth." (JOHN 17:17)

Yearling Bull, Fraser, Colorado, August 29, 2013

Mid-size, Winter Park, Colorado, September 17, 2018

Bull Moose: foreground shows where it rubbed velvet off its antlers. Snake River, Wyoming, August 6, 2007

With age, a bull moose becomes a mighty creature with huge antlers. But they are not born that way. Their antlers are small during the first year. Antlers are shed and each year and grow progressively larger over about six years. The normal pattern of growth seen throughout creation helps us to see that God made things to progress and mature. This is also true for man. God sanctifies His children by the preaching of His Word, enabling them to become more and more like His Son, Jesus, possessing more love, stronger faith, brighter hope, more joy and peace.

Moose can be found where there are abundant aquatic plants and aspen or willow twigs. They eat about 60 pounds of food a day. The deer kind, including moose, have two sets of hairs: the top layer of guard hair has air spaces inside. The air spaces help insulate their bodies and help to float their bodies in the water when they swim. The top layer, combined with the soft dense undercoat, enables moose to be comfortable in cold climates. Moose are thoughtfully made by the Creator.

"Splendor and majesty are before him [LORD]; strength and joy are in his place." (1 CHRONICLES 16:27)

Mule Deer Buck decides which way to move across the field, Franktown, Colorado, October 20, 2014

In the context of Scripture, the Creator's art has meaning and significance. The above scene of diverse life forms illustrates God's splendor. Each tree, bush and type of grass, fills a niche to make the place beautiful. Fall colors are a picture of joy and deer exhibit the strength and majesty of God.

Dear God, we see the glorious tapestry of creation and are grateful to realize its significance as a display of your might. The splendor of your plants and animals help us to know your greatness.

Mule Deer buck eating scrub oak leaves, Parker, Colorado, November 2, 2015

God is Good & Merciful

I sing the goodness of the Lord that
Filled the earth with food;
He formed the creatures with His Word
And then pronounced them good.
Lord, how Thy wonders are displayed
Where'er I turn my eye:
If I survey the ground I tread
Or gaze upon the sky!

—*I Sing The Mighty Power of God*, Isaac Watts, 1715

Mourning Dove, Madison, Wisconsin, February 8, 2018

"Hear, O my people … O Israel, … I am the LORD your God,
who brought you up out of the land of Egypt.
Open your mouth wide, and I will fill it." (PSALM 81: 8A-10)

Broad-Tailed Hummingbirds, Elizabeth, Colorado, August 7, 2017

God's steadfast love for us is exemplified by a mother bird and its chick as a living parable. The chick illustrates our dependence on God. With much faith in God's promises, our mouths are open wide to feed on His Word and to pour out our soul in prayer and praise. The God of mercy who brought His people out of Egypt is pleased to fill the mouth of the hungry soul with every good thing. He *"is able to do far more abundantly than all that we ask or think, according to the power at work within us"* (Ephesians 3:20).

"It is not good that man should be alone"

Why did God make beasts, livestock, birds, reptiles, fish, amphibians, insects, and dinosaurs?

"Then the LORD God said, It is not good that the man should be alone; I will make him a helper fit for him. So out of the ground the LORD God formed every beast of the field and every bird of the heavens and brought them to the man to see what he would call them. And whatever the man called every living creature, that was its name. The man gave names to all livestock and to the birds of the heavens and to every beast of the field." (GENESIS 2:18-19)

Creatures purposely enrich our lives. We are awestruck by a brightly colored hummingbird, a cute puppy, a soaring eagle, the controlled-strength of a horse, and the immensity of a whale leaping out of the ocean. We study them and name them. They satisfy our hearts with gladness, a witness to God's love for us. So we should leave space for wild plants and creatures.

"Woe to those who join house to house, who add field to field, until there is no more room, and you are made to dwell alone in the midst of the land." (ISAIAH 5:8)

The awareness of male and female of every animal likely gave Adam a clear picture of a helpmate. Then, when God made Eve, Adam recognized the helper fit for him "at last."

"But for Adam there was not found a helper fit for him ... And the rib that the LORD God had taken from the man he made into a woman and brought her to the man. Then the man said 'This at last is bone of my bones and flesh of my flesh; she shall be called Woman.'"

(GENESIS 2:20B, 22, 23A)

John holding Eclectus Parrots at Wildlife World, Litchfield Park, AZ, December 31, 2004

"Look at the birds of the air; they do not sow or reap or store away in barns, and yet your heavenly Father feeds them. Are you not much more valuable than they?" (MATTHEW 6:24)

Black Rosy Finch, Beartooth Plateau, WY, August 11, 2016

God's care for finches can assure us that He will meet our needs. He put diversity in the Finch kind so that they could adapt to wide areas of the world, including Australia and Africa. The black rosy finch lives among the tundra at 11,000 feet elevation in the mountains. There it has little competition for seeds. The rosy color in the black rosy finch's wing matches its surrounding and the black color helps it to absorb radiation from the sun for warmth. Be assured that the Maker of the birds supplies all that we need to give Him glory. *"He who did not spare his own Son but gave him up for us all, how will he not also with him graciously give us all things?"* (Romans 8:32)

"And should not I pity Nineveh, that great city, in which there are more than 120,000 persons who do not know their right hand from their left, and also much cattle?" (JONAH 4:11)

San Luis Valley, Colorado, May 2, 2015

God used Jonah to turn Niveveh from their wicked ways, despite Jonah's resistance to God's call. The animals were included in the reason God had compassion on Niveveh and were included in the fast that king proclaimed: *"Let neither man nor beast, herd nor flock, taste anything. Let them not feed or drink water, but let man and beast be covered with sackcloth, and let them call out mightily to God"* (Jonah 3:7-8). God forgave people who, with their animals, fasted and turned from their evil ways. Man's sin and repentance affects the lives of animals. *"And not only the creation, but we ourselves, who have the firstfruits of the Spirit, groan inwardly as we wait eagerly for adoption as sons, the redemption of our bodies"* (Romans 8:23).

"When the donkey saw the angel of the Lord, she lay down under Balaam." (NUMBERS 22:27)

Gray Squirrel, Sugar Creek Conservation Area, Kirksville, Missouri, January 1, 1980

Animals are probably able to sense more than we realize. I was sitting in a conservation area and this squirrel came along, nibbled on an acorn and then looked at me with obvious curiosity. Another time, I had a squirrel curiously come up behind me and purr. I did not know they had the same ability as cats to show affection. They are not made in the image of God as humans. But they often exhibit remarkable capabilities, often for our benefit, according to the sovereign will of God.

"The eyes of all look to you, and you give them their food in due season. You open your hand; you satisfy the desire of every living thing."
(PSALM 145:15-16)

Forest Above Deep Lake, Beartooth Plateau, Wyoming, August 15, 2017

The white-tailed ptarmigan is a mountain bird, related to grouse. God provided ptarmigan with feathers that are camouflage in the summer forest. The feathers turn white in the winter to blend in with the snow, satisfying its need to hide from predators. God filled mountain forests with grouse whortleberry berry plants to provide food for the ptarmigan. It is a blessing to see these birds. They are wonderful companions in the wilderness.

"The LORD is good to all, and his mercy is over all that he has made."

(PSALM 145:9)

Killdeer over camouflaged eggs, Weldon Springs Conservation Area, Weldon Springs, Missouri, April 16, 2008

An all-knowing and loving God enabled animals to survive in a sin-filled world. The killdeer bird was given the instinct to put its spotted eggs where they are perfectly camouflaged. Right after I took this picture, the bird danced progressively away from the eggs. It pretended to have a broken wing to distract me away from the nest. God is merciful to provide these protective means. He is also merciful to us by giving the shield of faith in Jesus. In Christ, we are free from the slavery to sin. We are also strengthened to love God, delight in His Word, live a godly life, be zealous for good works, and have hope in the return of Jesus and eternal life with God. *"Oh give thanks to the LORD, for he is good; for his steadfast love endures forever!"* (1 Chronicles 16:34)

"He [Christ] entered once for all into the holy places, not by means of the blood of goats and calves but by means of his own blood, thus securing an eternal redemption. ... offered himself without blemish ... Therefore he is the mediator of a new covenant, so that those who are called may receive the promised eternal inheritance." (HEBREWS 9:11B-12, 14B, 15A)

Sheep at Lost Branch Blueberry Farm, Kirksville, Missouri, May 8, 2010

Before Jesus' work on the cross, God commanded that His people sacrifice innocent and unblemished animals to atone for their sins. Death was God's judgement for sin. Oxen, rams, calves, lambs, goats, turtledoves, and pigeons were used as instructed by God's Word. The sacrifices including grain, were also to offer thanksgiving to God, receive peace, and see the glory of the Lord appear to them. The requirements were to prepare people for the time when the innocent Christ would shed His own blood on the cross, securing an eternal redemption for people from sin. Now with a sincere heart, Christians confess sins, pray, hear the preaching of the Word, and baptize. They remember as one body what Christ did for them on the cross and receive Him afresh by taking communion. Christians offer tithes, sing, and receive forgiveness for their sins by God's grace through faith in Jesus Christ.

"I am the good shepherd. I know my own and my own know me, just as the Father knows me and I know the Father; and I lay down my life for the sheep ... I give them eternal life, and they will never perish, and no one will snatch them out of my hand. My Father, who has given them to me, is greater than all, and no one is able to snatch them out of the Father's hand." (JOHN 10:11-18, 28-29)

Frontier Park, St. Charles, Missouri, May 22, 2005

Jesus alone made salvation (eternal life) possible for all of the children of God. He is known by them. No one will snatch them out of His hand (John 10:28). It is good news that we are in the hands of the good shepherd, who never loses any of His sheep.

"So Jesus again said to them, 'Truly, truly, I say to you, I am the door of the sheep. All who came before me are thieves and robbers, but the sheep did not listen to them. I am the door. If anyone enters by me, he will be saved and will go in and out and find pasture. The thief comes only to steal and kill and destroy. I came that they may have life and have it abundantly." (JOHN 10:7-10)

Peter and Thomas at Daniel Boone Village, Defiance, Missouri, May 10, 2004

Sheep are dependent upon the shepherd just as we are dependent on Jesus. When the shepherd speaks, the sheep know that they should follow because his ways are better than their ways. They do not listen or follow others who are thieves and robbers.

Dear God, thank you for sending your Son that we may have an abundant life in Him as our Shepherd.

"You are a hiding place for me; you preserve me from trouble; you surround me with shouts of deliverance." (PSALM 32:7)

Black-Tailed Jackrabbit in a our Meadow, Elizabeth, Colorado, August 1, 2017

Jackrabbits are comfortable in our meadow. By God's mercy, hares know to hide among the tall grass and yucca. Their long back legs enable them to leap high in the air and run 40 miles per hour if needed. They feed in the evening and night-time hours when they are less visible. Instead of prairie grass and leaping abilities, God's children are surrounded by His promises and examples in history of His saving protection. *"King Darius wrote to all the peoples … he is the living God, … He delivers and rescues; … he who has saved Daniel from the power of the lions"* (Daniel 6:26-27).

God is Sovereign

There's not a plant or flower
Below but makes Thy glories known;
And clouds arise and tempests
Blow by order from Thy throne;
While all that borrows life
From Thee is ever in Thy care;
And everywhere that man can be,
Thou, God, are present there.

—*I Sing The Mighty Power of God*, Isaac Watts, 1715

"O Lord my God, you are very great!
... you water the mountains ...
The high mountains are for the wild goats."
(PSALM 104:1,13,18)

Mountain Goat, Gray's Peak,
July 4, 2015

"Praise your God, O Zion! ... He sends out his command to the earth; his word runs swiftly. He gives snow like wool; he scatters frost like ashes. ... He declares his word to Jacob, his statutes and rules to Israel. He has not dealt thus with any other nation; they do not know his rules."

(PSALM 147:12B,15-16, 19-20)

Mule Deer, Parker, Colorado, November 16, 2015

God's commands to the earth are effective according to the will of His pleasure. Plants survive, deer quench their thirst, and His people are guided in the ways of life. The order of the universe is under God's control. In the face of God's sovereignty and steadfast love, we can trust His promises and confidently walk in His ways. *"Blessed are the people to whom such blessings fall! Blessed are the people whose God is the LORD!"* (Psalm 144:15)

"The voice of the Lord makes the deer give birth and strips the forests bare, and in his temple all cry, 'Glory!'" (PSALM 29:9)

Mule Deer, Elizabeth, Colorado, July 11, 2011

Deer illustrate that God made all things and upholds them. I was touched to see this mule deer nursing her fawn. Why do the fawns know to seek their mother's milk? Why does the mother care for her young? An answer is that God made the deer's instincts for His glory. We learn that Christ, being the exact imprint of God's nature, *"upholds the universe by the word of his power"* (Hebrews 1:3). Christ the Lord is sovereign over all that He made including deer, forests and us!

Dear God, we delight to do your will, and proclaim your goodness. We know that your everlasting kingdom will be established with a place for all who respond in faith.

"Do you know when the mountain goats give birth? Do you observe the calving of the does? Can you number the months that they fulfill, and do you know the time when they give birth, when they crouch, bring forth their offspring, and are delivered of their young? Their young ones become strong; they grow up in the open; they go out and do not return to them." (JOB 39:1-4)

Female Big Horn Sheep and Kid, Empire, Colorado, August 8, 2015

Wild goats of the mountains are the Ibex and the related mountain goat, Dall, and bighorn sheep. They are gifted by God to be at home in the high mountains. Not only did He give them the genetic potential to thrive there, but He also sustains them as He watches over every detail of their existence. And so they have existed for thousands of years. How much more will God sustain those He created in His own image for His glory? By His grace He *"acts for those who wait for him"* (Isaiah 64:4b).

"O Lord, how manifold are your works! In wisdom have you made them all; the earth is full of your creatures. Here is the sea, great and wide, which teems with creatures innumerable, living things both small and great." (PSALM 104:24-25)

Red Knob Sea Star

Lion Fish

Juvenile French Angel Fish, Denver Zoo, April 11, 2018

The plants and creatures of the oceans are vast and made in wisdom as Scripture proclaimed about 3,000 years ago (Psalm 104). God rejoices in His creatures because they make His glory and wisdom known. *"May the glory of the Lord endure forever; may the Lord rejoice in his works"* (Psalm 104:31).

"For every beast of the forest is mine, the cattle on a thousand hills."
(PSALM 50:10)

Longhorn steer, Elbert, Colorado, July 27, 2017

Everything we have comes from God, and at the highest level, its purpose is to give Him glory. He owns all animals in the wild and on every ranch. He does not need anything, including our sacrifices. *"For I desire steadfast love and not sacrifice, the knowledge of God rather than burnt offerings"* (Hosea 6:6).

"I know all the birds of the hills." (PSALM 50:11)

Mountain Bluebird on a frosty morning, Elizabeth, Colorado, April 24, 2018

The Maker of the birds knows all the birds. This is beyond human comprehension. However, it is for us to know, as the Holy Spirit enables it, as an illustration of the divine nature of God. Only He is God, and we are not. The keratin layer of a male bird's feathers contains bubbles of air made in a precise way so that blue-light bounces off the bubbles and scatter back into the air, and other colors scatter randomly or are absorbed. Why did God make the air cells as the source of color? Maybe He protected birds from becoming a substrate for blue pigment factories. He knows the thoughts of man and considers all things from the beginning. *"Praise the Lord ... flying birds ... kings of the earth and all peoples, princes and all rulers of the earth! ... Let them praise the name of the Lord, for his name alone is exalted; his majesty is above earth and heaven"* (Psalm 148:1a,10b,11,13).

"Is it by your understanding that the hawk soars and spreads his wings toward the south?" (JOB 39:26)

Swainson's Hawk, Elizabeth, Colorado, May 5, 2018

A Swainson's hawk dove from the sky over my car with its wings tucked in and landed on a post nearby. What a stunning bird. I did some research and learned that this hawk is known for its long migration to Argentina in the winter and its diet of grasshoppers there. I wondered why does this bird fly so far in the winter? I found the answer in the book of Job: to help us know that God is sovereign.

"Is it at your command that the eagle mounts up and makes his nest on high? On the rock he dwells and makes his home, on the rocky crag and stronghold. From there he spies out the prey; his eyes behold it from far away." (JOB 39:27-29)

Sea Eagle, Denver Zoo, Colorado, November 3, 2017

Eagles are gifted with keen eyesight, enabling them to find food as they soar high in the air. They use thermal updrafts to carry them upward. This behavior, according to God's will, is a living parable of our life in Jesus. He gifts us with what we need to serve Him and lifts us in His strength to do it. *"As each has received a gift, use it … as one who serves by the strength that God supplies"* (1 Peter 4:10).

"You [Elijah] shall drink from the brook, and I have commanded the ravens to feed you there. ... And the ravens brought him bread and meat in the morning and bread and meat in the evening, and he drank from the brook." (1 KINGS 17:4,6)

Ravens, Grand Canyon, Arizona, January 3, 2005

The sovereign God commanded ravens to feed Elijah. His sovereignty and compassion for animals was also exhibited when He drew the animals to the ark that Noah built. God also closed the door after the animals were all in. *"Of the birds according to their kinds, and of the animals according to their kinds, of every creeping thing of the ground, according to its kind, two of every sort shall come in to you to keep them alive"* (Genesis 6:19-21).

"From eternity to eternity You are God"

(PSALM 90:2)

The more I meditate on God, the more I feel like Job and Agur, who after studying His creation humbly, expressed how limited they are in grasping the totality of God.

"I have not learned wisdom, nor have I knowledge of the Holy One. Who has ascended to heaven and come down? Who has gathered the wind in his fists? Who has wrapped up the waters in a garment? Who has established all the ends of the earth? What is his name, and what is his son's name? Surely you know!"

(PROVERBS 30:3-4)

There is a place for every creature, with the food and environment it needs to thrive. At the same time the creatures contribute to the habitat by pollenating and distributing seeds. Thus, together plants and animals have been sustained for thousands of years. By the infinite wisdom of the living God they help us to know His power, goodness, and glory.

This Western Tanager in Wyoming is colored like the flowers of this wooded meadow that also supplies it with food, shelter, and trees for its nest—all in place according to the will of God for His glory.

Pebble Creek Trail, Yellowstone national Park, Wyoming, August 1, 2008

Gloria teaching Nathanael about minnows and frogs, water and grass, flowers and rocks. All of God's creation is significant, inspiring young minds.

Leigh Lake, Teton National Park, Wyoming, August 20, 2010

The sky-blue eyes, textured-white feathers, shinny-orange beak, and excellent parenting skills of the Embden goose are a testimony of God's infinite wisdom.

Sunset Regional Park, Las Vegas, Nevada, October 22, 2018

Mergansers, Leigh Lake, Teton Nation Park, August 14, 2016

WALK HUMBLY
with God

"What does your God require?"

How can one respond to God's saving grace and love? The Spirit compels God's children to obey Him, seek His ways, and walk with Him, abiding in Jesus and His Word by faith. This is the Christian life. The study of creation and Scripture causes one to be increasingly more humble before the almighty and infinite God. The Christian loves insight and truth. Insights are the work of the Holy Spirit and faith in Jesus. God's Word is not to be read and put aside; it is to be applied to every aspect of life.

"And now, Israel, what does the LORD your God require of you, but to fear the LORD your God, to walk in all his ways, to love him, to serve the LORD your God with all your heart and with all your soul, and to keep the commandments and statues of the LORD ... Behold, to the LORD your God belong heaven and ... the earth with all that is in it. Yet the LORD ... chose ... you above all peoples, as you are this day."
(DEUTERONOMY 10:12-15)

"He has told you, O man, what is good; and what does the LORD require of you but to do justice, and to love kindness, and to walk humbly with your God?" (MICAH 6:8)

"Your attitude should be the same as that of Christ Jesus: Who, being in very nature God, did not consider equality with God something to be grasped, but made himself nothing, taking the very nature of a servant, being made in human likeness. And being found in appearance as a man, he humbled himself and became obedient to death – even death on a cross!"
(PHILIPPIANS 2:5-8)

"For it is no empty word for you, but your very life."
(DEUTERONOMY 32:47)

Bison abide in grasslands, trout in cold streams, and eagles in the air. Christians are most at home when they abide in Jesus and His Word. Jesus is preparing a place for them where He is, in His Father's house.

Hayden Valley, Yellowstone National Park, August 18, 2010

Ceaseless Praise to God

Take my life, and let it be consecrated, Lord, to thee.
Take my moments and my days;
Let them flow in ceaseless praise,
Let them flow in ceaseless praise.

—*Take My Life, and Let It Be*, Frances Ridley Havergal, 1843

Western Meadowlark, Elizabeth, Colorado,
May 29, 2017

"All the earth worships you and sings praises to you; they sing praises to your name." (PSALM 66:4)

Male Northern Flicker, Elizabeth, Colorado, April 9, 2018

A flicker sang on our rooftop one morning. Such a beautiful example of how to start the day! I saw these birds poking their beaks into the ground and learned that ants are their main food. They use a long barbed tongue to collect the ants from the dirt. Their bib, spotted breast, and wing pattern tells that our Creator likes design!

Dear God, we sing praises to you for surrounding us with beauty.

"Even the sparrow finds a home, and the swallow a nest for herself, where she may lay her young, at your altars, O Lord of hosts, my King and my God. Blessed are those who dwell in your house, ever singing your praise! Selah." (PSALM 84:3-4)

Tree Swallows celebrate their ability to fly from the nest; Pike's Peak in background. Elizabeth, Colorado, July 9, 2018

Birds seek homes to raise their young. This is a metaphor of a Christian's desire to dwell with God as they raise children to know Him in Jesus. Servants of Jesus long to take communion and sing praises in the house of God. Through this worship, Christians are blessed!

"Sing to the Lord with thanksgiving; make melody to our God on the lyre! He covers the heavens with clouds; he prepares rain for the earth; he makes grass grow on the hills. He gives to the beasts their food, and to the young ravens that cry. His delight is not in the strength of the horse, nor his pleasure in the legs of a man, but the Lord takes pleasure in those who fear him, in those who hope in his steadfast love." (PSALM 147:7-11)

Bison Calf, Thermopolis, Wyoming, May 28, 2016

Sing to God with thanksgiving for His blessings in the land. Our thanksgivings tend to focus on our health and family. But Psalm 147 reminds us to be grateful for rain, grass, beasts and ravens in the wilderness. Why? Because they are expressions of God's glory. Praise God for giving food to the young bison. He is made in wisdom to live in a herd in the Great Plains! The bison please the eye and helped settlers of the land to survive.

"Praise the LORD from the earth, you great sea creatures and all deeps." (PSALM 148:7)

Powder Blue Tang Fish in front of a large clam, Denver Zoo, Colorado, April 11, 2018

Brightly colored large salt-water clams, sea anemone, and Powder Blue Tang fish of coral reefs praise the Creator with bright colors and swaying movements. The brown colors of the clam's tissues and sea anemone are caused by pigments of photosynthetic algae from which they get sugars to live. The electric blue spots in the clam tissue contain nanometer-sized lattices that direct the needed blue and red wavelengths to the algae, while reflecting the rest to avoid overheating. God assigned life-giving functions to the colors that praise Him.

"Praise the Lord! ... praise him in the heights!"
(PSALM 148:1B)

Female Clubhorned Grasshopper, Parry Peak, Colorado, September, 17, 2018

A green grasshopper was sunning itself on a rock above the tree line on Parry Peak Mountain, Colorado. It seems that God included in the genetics of grasshoppers the ability to have stunted wing growth so they can praise Him in the heights. This trait likely enables the insect to mature more quickly and thereby complete its lifecycle during the brief time of warmth in the alpine environment. Its diet likely includes lichen (fungi) on the rocks.

"Let everything that has breath praise the Lord! Praise the Lord!"
(PSALM 150:6)

Nuttall's Blister Beetle, Elizabeth, Colorado, June 9, 2018

Nuttall's blister beetles praise God with iridescent colors. They have breath. Beetles breathe air and remove carbon dioxide with the inflation and deflation of tracheal tubes hooked up to pores along its body (Hochgraf, JS, 2018). Blister beetles get their name because a touch of its body causes it to ooze a toxic, oily substance called cantharidin that blisters the skin. Praise the LORD for all of the creative ways that He protects His creatures. *"The LORD is good to all, and his mercy is over all that he has made"* (Psalm 145:9).

"Great are the works of the LORD, studied by all who delight in them."

(PSALM 111:2)

Aberrant version of Polaris Fritillary (Boloria polaris), Beartooth Plateau, Wyoming, August 13, 2017

Seek God and He will open your eyes to many glorious things that are otherwise overlooked. Above is an apparent rare fritillary butterfly photographed while on an all-day hike in the wilderness. It would be easy to walk right by this small creature while seeking a personal achievement. Notice also the colorful collection of arctic plants. Help your children to take their time and thirst to see what God puts before them so they can know His greatness. Consider what God may be saying through the discoveries by searching His Word. Then tell others what you are learning with ceaseless praises to God for revealing it to you. His grace fills our lives with pleasures forever!

"Three things are too wonderful for me; four I do not understand: the way of an eagle in the sky, the way of a serpent on a rock, the way of a ship on the high seas, and the way of a man with a virgin."

(PROVERBS 30:18-19)

Garter snake, August A. Busch Memorial Conservation Area, Weldon Springs, Missouri, September 4, 2006

The creation of animals and humans, including their behavior, is beyond comprehension. It humbles us before the God who created all things and encourages us to praise Him.

Live in the Spirit

DOING GOOD WORKS FOR GOD

Take my hands, and let them move
At the impulse of thy love.
Take my feet, and let them be
Swift and beautiful for thee,
Swift and beautiful for thee.

—*Take My Life, and Let It Be*, Frances Ridley Havergal, 1843

Expose children to donkeys to help them see humble servanthood

Missouri, October 11, 2004

"Make me know the way I should go, for to you I lift up my soul...
Teach me to do your will, for you are my God!
Let your good Spirit lead me on level ground!" (PSALM 143:8B,10)

Elizabash Parade, Elizabeth, Colorado, June 1, 2012

Help children to trust God by enabling them to have the experience of seeing how a horse trusts them as a rider. Horses are powerful and also timid. They trust a child and surrender their will to a child's requests as they see the benefits of the child's guidance and love. The rider is satisfied when the horse surrenders its will because the result is a successful journey. This experience may help children to appreciate that the potential to do good works requires trust in our master. Trusting God is most encouraging because God is perfect in patience, steadfast in love, and promises everlasting life through faith in Jesus. He lifts up our souls.

"For by grace you have been saved through faith. And this is not your own doing; it is the gift of God, not a result of works, so that no one may boast. For we are his workmanship, created in Christ Jesus for good works, which God prepared beforehand, that we should walk in them."

(EPHESIANS 2:8-9)

Homestead Harvest Days, Highland, Illinois, September 8, 2007

Isn't this a beautiful sight? The horses are pleased to work together. They serve their owner as they were trained. All this as purposed by God who made the owners and the horses to work the land and keep it. There is a special pleasure in doing what God has called us to do. The horses get better and better at serving their master. They much prefer work to being idle. In the strength of Christ, we also progressively die to self and live more and more for God. This is not something that we do alone, but in the strength of Jesus and with the partnership and prayers of the church body. Like a team of horses, we seek to work in unity of mind with others in the church to bring glory to God in Christ Jesus.

"She seeks wool and flax, and works with willing hands." (PROVERBS 31:13)

Reenactment at Historic Daniel Boone Home, Defiance, Missouri, May 1, 2005

Fort Massac Reenactment, Illinois, October 22, 2006

Sheep wool was made by God as good material for clothes. It takes willing hands to shear sheep and prepare the fibers. Sheep are willing to have their wool sheared without resistance when all is done in loving relationships between animals and people. The resulting clothes protect people from the cold and reflect their character.

When we put on our clothes, we can be reminded to put on Christ. He offers Himself without resistance to those who love Him.

"As for me and my house, we will serve the LORD." (JOSHUA 24:15B)

The egg was about the size of a navy bean, June 24, 2017

Mother Hummingbird carefully feeding her chick, July 22, 2017

Birds instinctively build nests in trees (Psalm 104:17) to protect the next generation from predators and direct sunlight. Their nests are well attached and insulated with mud, mulch, and dog fur, woven together with seed heads and camouflaged with lichen. The process requires hundred of trips. After a chick is born, the mother feeds it, protects it, and encourages it to follow its God-given instincts.

What the birds illustrate by instinct, we can do all the more in the strength of Christ, and the power of the Holy Spirit, for God's glory. We build our homes with thousands of trips to His Word. The homes are insulated with prayer and decorated with worship to God. We encourage the next generation to know God and walk in His ways.

"Three things are stately in their tread; four are stately in their stride: the lion, which is mightiest among beasts and does not turn back before any; the strutting rooster, the he-goat, and a king whose army is with him."

(PROVERBS 30:29-31)

Denver Zoo, November 3, 2017

Agur studied God's creation and noticed fearless creatures and a king with his army. I can speak from my own experience that a rooster is majestic and fearless in serving as a protector of hens. The bright red comb on the rooster's head and the wattle and earlobes below proclaim that he is the guard of the flock. When approached, he struts back and forth in front of the hens. In defensive posture, the hairs around his neck extend straight out and he quickly flutters in the air with his spurs extended to make contact. It is an awe-inspiring show. The brightly colored, iridescent feathers and showy tail design are majestic. When something is up, his loud voice, like a lions roar, is sounded several times rather than retreat.

Roosters, lions, and he-goats illustrate how we can be confident in our calling. Let us humbly embrace our God-given roles. When we respect those Jesus puts above us, we acknowledge that He is above us with all authority in heaven and earth. He gives some of us authority as husbands and parents, and in Christ, we can protect and disciple those in our care with a hint of His majesty and fearlessness. These characteristics will help the next generation to know that Christ is alive and strengthen us to walk in His ways. Our courage is a witness to the world that acts in fear (of man, creation, death). May others be drawn to Jesus through our witness. In this way, we build the kingdom of God on earth, teaching everything Jesus commanded.

Elizabeth, Colorado, January 4, 2018

"Are not five sparrows sold for two pennies? And not one of them is forgotten before God. Why, even the hairs of your head are all numbered. Fear not; you are of more value than many sparrows." (LUKE 12:6-7)

White-Cowned Sparrow, Crested Butte, Colorado, July 11, 2017

I went through a time in graduate school when my hope in academic excellence suffered and I lost a sense of value. My anxiety was great before a physical chemistry exam and a friend, Todd Gusek, put the following verse on my desk and shared that it had been helpful to him: *"Do not be anxious about anything, but in everything by prayer and supplication with thanksgiving let your requests be made known to God. And the peace of God, which surpasses all understanding, will guard your hearts and your minds in Christ Jesus"* (Philippians 4:6-7). The Holy Spirit used these words to convict me that my heart was not right. I repented of my sins and turned my heart to Jesus. From then on, I was assured that I was a child of God, forever valuable in His sight. Praise God for His grace.

"Drink water from your own cistern, flowing water from your own well. ... Let your fountain be blessed, and rejoice in the wife of your youth, a lovely deer, a graceful doe. ... For a man's ways are before the eyes of the LORD and he ponders all his paths." (PROVERBS 5:18-19, 21)

Parker, Colorado, December 3, 2015

A man who rejoices in his wife is blessed by God. We can see in creation, as God said in His Word, that He made male and female related, different, and both essential. A doe illustrates the preciousness of one's wife: someone to cherish and honor with faithfulness. This honor is also wise before the eyes of God who judges. *"Let marriage be held in honor among all, and let the marriage bed be undefiled, for God will judge the sexually immoral and adulterous"* (Hebrews 13:4). *"You shall not commit adultery"* (Exodus 20:14).

"To the married I give this charge (not I, but the Lord): the wife should not separate from her husband (but if she does, she should remain unmarried or else be reconciled to her husband), and the husband should not divorce his wife." (1 CORINTHIANS 7:10)

Swan Couple in Bruges, Belgium, October 8, 2004

In God's providence, swans make a heart shape with their necks as they face each other during courtship. Mating couples typically stay together for life. Though not perfect in illustration, swans are a picture of the beauty of biblical truth.

Dear God, We know that we can be faithful to our spouses by the power of Jesus and the Holy Spirit in us, to our benefit and your glory. May we illustrate your beauty and grace in our marriages.

"Husbands love your wives, as Christ loved the church and gave himself up for her, that he might sanctify her."
(EPHESIANS 5:25-26A)

Ringed-Neck Doves, Elizabeth, Colorado, July 4, 2018

Husbands, love your wives with the affection Christ has for His church. One can read the following verse as a metaphor where Christ speaks of the church as His dove: *"Arise, my love, my beautiful one, and come away; ... O my dove ... let me hear your voice, for your voice is sweet, and your face is lovely"* (Song of Solomon 2:10,14).

"Then God said, 'Let us make mankind in our image, in our likeness, so that they may rule over the fish in the sea, over the livestock and all the wild animals, and over all the creatures that move along the ground.'" (GENESIS 1:26)

"And God said to them, 'be fruitful and multiply and fill the earth and subdue it.'" (GENESIS 2:28)

Dry land was irrigated to raise cattle, August 14, 2010

We were made in God's image. Therefore we have a responsibility to subdue the earth and care for the living things that move on the earth. Here we see an example of a farmer who turned a dry land into a green pasture, a healthy place to raise cattle.

"If you meet your enemy's ox or his donkey going astray, you shall bring it back to him." (EXODUS 23:4)

Fort Massac Encampment, Metropolis, Illinois, June 3, 2006

Made in God's image, we are to have dominion over animals. It is appropriate to train animals to help us work the land. *"The oxen were plowing"* (Job 1:14b). The dominion task also involves caring for the animals. Seek to protect animals, control their potential for harm, and help them give God glory with the abilities God gave them. If an oxen has gone astray, one should return the animal to his owner, even if that owner is an enemy.

"Whoever is righteous has regard for the life of his beast, but the mercy of the wicked is cruel." (PROVERBS 12:10)

Goldendoodle named "Prince William of Orange," October 15, 2011

Cat named "General Thomas Jackson" and my wife, Lida, October 3, 2015

Praise God for the gift of pets. Cats and dogs are helpful for teaching children responsibility and to see love and acceptance modeled by them. My experience is that dogs illustrate a consistent picture of enthusiasm and love even if it is only for a treat, and not of the Spirit. Animals can illustrate the actions of love because they were made by God to be this way for our benefit. *"The earth is full of the steadfast love of the LORD"* (Psalm 33:5b). We are to have regard for the life of our pets, fowl, and livestock as special gifts from God.

"And God blessed Noah and his sons … Every moving thing that lives shall be food for you. And as I gave you the green plants, I give you everything. But you shall not eat flesh with its life, that is, its blood. … Noah began to be a man of the soil, and he planted a vineyard." (GENESIS 9:1A,3-4,20)

Red mark on the Cutthroat trout is a reminder of the blood involved in preparing flesh as food, Deep Lake, Wyoming, August 12, 2016

After the global flood, God told Noah and his sons that in addition to every plant created for food (not poisonous plants), they could now also eat every animal created for food (not cats and dogs). Noah was instructed to take 7 pairs of each clean animal aboard the ark, some for sacrifice and some for food. Killing an animal and removing the blood and guts is not the same as picking apples, grapes, and walnuts. Noah was quick to produce plant foods, *"a man of the soil"* (Genesis 9:20). Except for survival, meat was a luxury, consumed at a special time of thanksgiving. *"And bring the fattened calf and kill it, and let us eat and celebrate. For this my son was dead, and is alive again; he was lost, and is found.' And they began to celebrate"* (Luke 15:21-24). Limiting meat consumption is wise as it typically still contains heme iron, especially in hamburger and steak (Cross AJ et al., 2012). Heme iron, but not iron from plants, contributes to heart disease, diabetes and cancer (Hunnicutt, J et al. 2014; Bao, W et al. 2012; Fonesca-Nunes, A et al. 2014). *"Be not among drunkards or among gluttonous eaters of meat"* (Proverbs 23:20).

"Whatever goes on its belly, and whatever goes on all fours, or whatever has many feet, any swarming thing that swarms on the ground, you shall not eat, for they are detestable. ... For I am the LORD your God. Consecrate yourselves therefore, and be holy, for I am holy." (LEVITICUS 11:42,44)

Short-Horned Lizard, Dawson Butte, Colorado, April 25, 2015

According to the Creator-God, one should not eat lizards. He made their appearance and habits to pour out speech that says, "do not eat me." Divisions between animals were known by Noah (Genesis 7:2) as a principle of life thousands of years before the covenant with Israel. Today we know that detestable attributes of lizards include parasites, pathogenic bacteria, viruses, and biotoxins (Magnine S et al. 2009). Rushdoony wrote "with reference to our health, the rules of diet are still valid rules. We do not observe the sabbath of Israel, but we do observe the Lord's day. We do not regard the kosher legislation as law today, but we do observe it as a sound rule for health.... Our observance of these dietary rules should never be to place a barrier between ourselves and other men but for our health and prosperity in Christ" (Rushdoony, 1972).

"The camel, because it chews the cud
but does not part the hoof, is unclean to you."
(LEVITICUS 11:4)

The camel has two large nails but does not walk on them. It walks on pads like cats and dogs.

Dear God, Thank you for making animals with distinct features for our benefit.

Camel's toes, Estes Park, Colorado, September 10, 2011

Pika, Deep Lake, Wyoming, August 12, 2016

"What father among you, if his son asks for a fish, will instead of a fish give him a serpent; or if he asks for an egg, will give him a scorpion?"

(LUKE 11:11-12)

Ameraucana and Rhode Island Red chicken eggs provided a mix of colored egg shells, May 10, 2012

We are to be kind and considerate in selecting special meals for our children. It is good to fulfill their wishes for fish and eggs, and unkind to replace those options with "detestable" ones, like serpents and scorpions (Leviticus 11:42, page 79).

"Test everything; hold fast what is good.
Abstain from every form of evil." (1 THESSALONIANS 5:21-22)

"Beloved, do not believe every spirit, but test the spirits to see whether they are from God, for many false prophets have gone out into the world. By this you know the Spirit of God: every spirit that confesses that Jesus Christ has come in the flesh is from God, and every spirit that does not confess Jesus is not from God." (1 JOHN 4:1-3A)

Female and male brook trout, Deep Lake, Beartooth Plateau, Wyoming, August 12, 2016

It is a privilege to see clear cold water and trout that live there. Trout are discerning about what they eat and where they live. In the lake where I caught these trout I used a popper that imitated a minnow, which typically swims to the surface to escape a feeding fish. In the mountains of Wyoming, the trout are active in mid-August and the male fish develop orange colored bellies and fins. Apparently God gave males the ability to produce these colors to impress discriminating females seeking the right mates to fertilize their eggs. Praise God who made the trout to be careful to discern what is good or false. Let us be encouraged to test the spirits in our walk with God, selecting to live in the healthy environment of God's grace, feeding on the real food of His Word.

The tiny green sweat bee propagates plants, like this Scarlet Globe-Mallow, through pollination and awes us with its metallic color as expressions of the Creator-God's steadfast love.

Elizabeth, Colorado, June 14, 2017

"Bless the Lord, O my soul,
and forget not all His benefits."
(PSALM 103:2)

God satisfies His creatures and us with good. For example, from Psalm 103:2-5 we learn that He:

- forgives all our iniquities
- heals all our diseases
- redeems us of our life from the pit
- crowns us with steadfast love and mercy
- satisfies us with good

Is there anything more valuable in all of life?

What is our response but to serve Him and tell others about the source of our joy!

"Only fear the LORD and serve him faithfully with all your heart.
For consider what great things he has done for you."
(1 SAMUEL 12:24)

"You make known to me the path of life; in your presence
there is fullness of joy; at your right hand
are pleasures forevermore." (PSALM 16:11)

Mature Merganser family preening their feathers by their God-given instinct to keep healthy. Big Horn River, Thermopolis, Wyoming, August 13, 2017

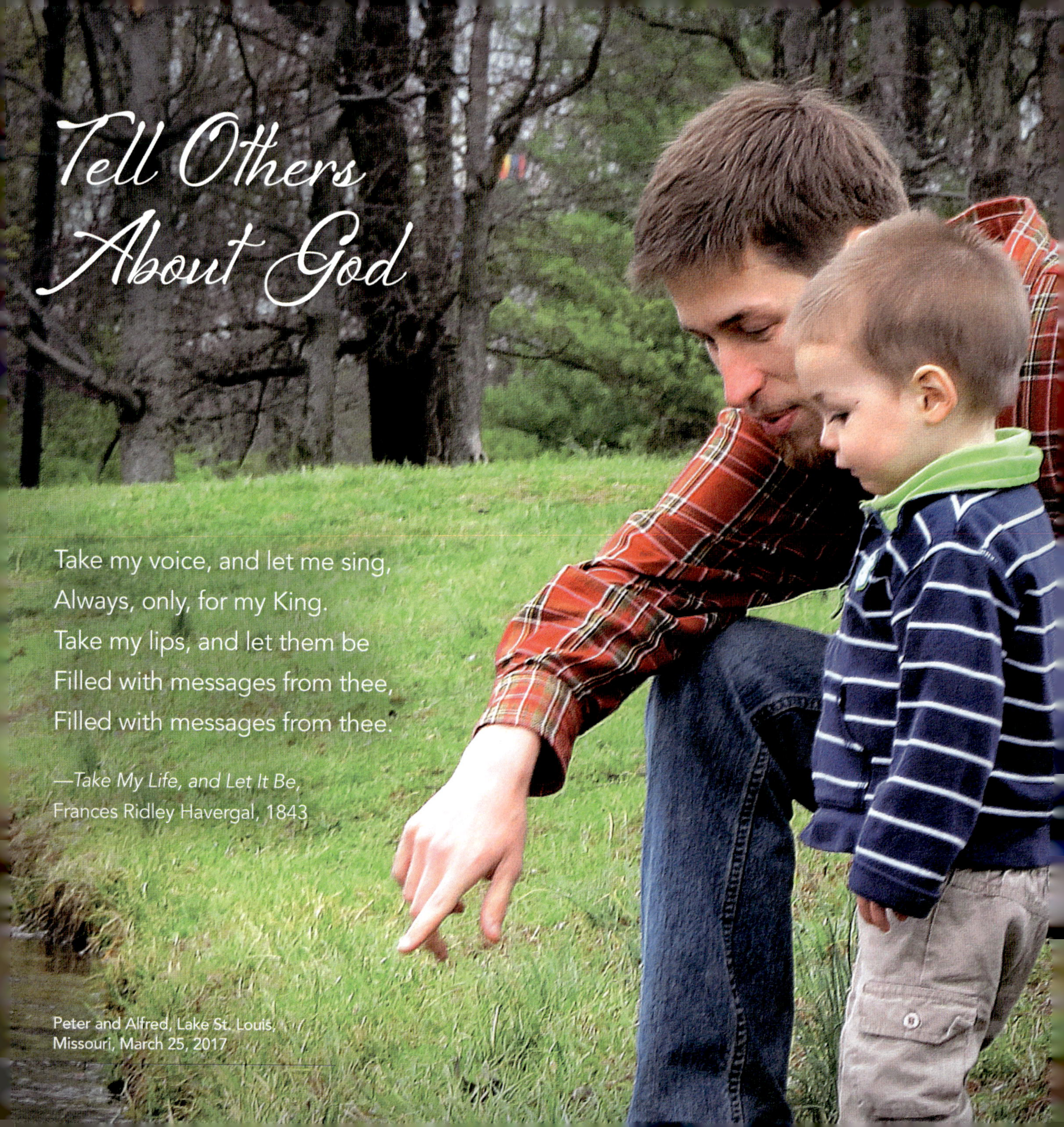

Tell Others About God

Take my voice, and let me sing,
Always, only, for my King.
Take my lips, and let them be
Filled with messages from thee,
Filled with messages from thee.

—*Take My Life, and Let It Be,*
Frances Ridley Havergal, 1843

Peter and Alfred, Lake St. Louis,
Missouri, March 25, 2017

"Therefore, knowing the fear of the Lord, we persuade others... the love of Christ controls us ... If anyone is in Christ, he is a new creation. The old has passed away; behold the new has come." (2 CORINTHIANS 5:17B)

Two-Tailed Tiger Swallowtail larva, September 4, 2016

Two-Tailed Tiger Swallowtail, June 23, 2016

In Christ, we are a new creation that is motivated by the love of Christ. We can use butterflies to illustrate this concept. God made the caterpillar to transform into a chrysalis and then emerge as a butterfly such as the two-tailed Tiger Swallowtail. The mature caterpillar looks like a serpent, a sign of the curse that came as a result of Adam's sin in the Garden of Eden. If you touch it, it puffs up its head, raises it, and sways it back and forth as if to warn of a strike. It can also stick out a forked appendage that looks like a snakes tongue. But it is harmless. I believe that God gave these characteristics to this creature to illustrate to us the self-seeking life apart from Christ. The caterpillar must die to itself and hang from a thread to be transformed by the grace of God, into a butterfly, a new creation that is set free to fly about to pollenate flowers, create a new generation, and illustrate God's goodness and beauty. This is a living parable of the life of a Christian. By the grace of God, and the power of the Holy Spirit through the preaching of God's word, we die to self and are set free in Christ to live in Him for God's glory.

"And these words that I command you today shall be on your heart. You shall teach them diligently to your children, and shall talk of them when you sit in your house, and when you walk by the way, and when you lie down, and when you rise." (DEUTERONOMY 6:7)

Giant Swallowtail Butterflies, Weldon Springs, Missouri, August 4, 2010

I am convicted by God's Word that we need to tell the next generation about God's works. Certainly, we should share how God parted the sea for the people of Israel to save them from Pharaoh's chariots, and horsemen by the faith of Moses (Exodus 14). It is also good for us to be with children so they can see us react to everyday observations of God's works with the truths of God's word. Imagine being with a young person observing a giant swallowtail butterfly. These are opportunities to tell them that the artwork of the wings proclaims the order, beauty, and goodness of God. Proclaim the truth. It was fascinating for our family to watch a courting pair of giant swallowtail butterflies, one within the fold of the upper side of the other, circle and spiral upward together into the sky. God is creative in making each creature unique in appearance and behavior. Every species of life can stop us in our tracks and invoke wonder. At these moments we need to say that this is just a hint of what life will be like with Jesus in heaven and in the new earth. Our children need to see that God's creation is not an end to itself. Creatures help us to know God in the context of Scripture. They are part of growing in our faith and enjoying God (Colossians 3:1-4).

"And he said to them, 'Follow me, and I will make you fishers of men.'"
(MATTHEW 4:19)

Peter, now a pastor, catching a trout, Snake River, Wyoming, August 8, 2007

Fishing takes perseverance and patience. One needs to learn about the fish and laboriously enter their environment. The fisherman skillfully presents the fly and watches for signs of the fish taking it. He holds the line tight and carefully lands the fish. In fishing for men the goal is to save their souls in Christ and expand the kingdom of God. The Christian shares the Word of God about Jesus and the Holy Spirit does the catching. New Christians are held tight as they are landed into *"the household of God, which is the church of the living God, a pillar and buttress of the truth"* (1 Timothy 3:15).

Dear God, give us faith that you have people for us to catch. Bless us with the spirit to abide with Jesus so He can work in us to expand your kingdom and glorify your name.

American Flamingo, Wildlife Word, Litchfield Park, Arizona, December 28, 2013

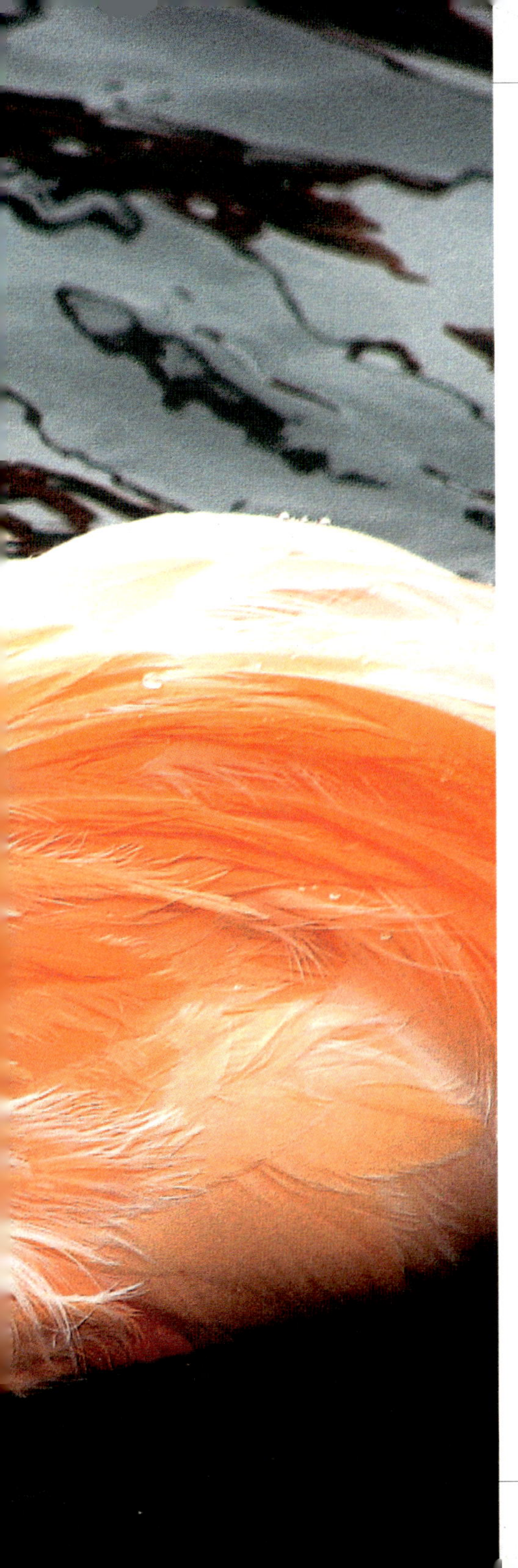

"Keep your conduct among the Gentiles honorable, so that when they speak against you as evildoers, they may see your good deeds and glorify God on the day of visitation."
(1 PETER 2:12)

God created the flamingo with the ability to filter tiny food particles such as algae from water and mud within its beak. Carotenoids from algae, including canthaxanthin, are the source of bright color in the birds feathers, legs, and beak. So a flamingo, functioning in the ways God planned, is beautiful, helping us to know His goodness.

God also made us to be attractive as we walk in His ways, even in specific ways that He planned for us individually. Our humble walk can be used by God to draw others to Him. Each of us have ways to exhibit holiness, faith, confidence, zeal, humility, wisdom of God, sincerity, perseverance, patience, love and servanthood. This walk contrasts with lives of worldliness, unbelief, despair, indifference and selfishness. This drawing of people by God will be in His timing. It may be on a day He visits with a wonder, a trial, or crisis. What satisfaction to think that others may respond with faith, based on our example in Christ.

Submit to God

Take my love; my Lord, I pour
At Thy feet its treasure-store.
Take myself, and I will be ever, only,
All for Thee, ever, only, all for Thee.

—*Take My Life, and Let It Be*, Frances Ridley Havergal, 1843

Isle Royale, Michigan, August 16, 2006

"Then Jesus told his disciples, If anyone would come after me, let him deny himself and take up his cross and follow me. For whoever would save his life will lose it, but whoever loses his life for my sake will find it."

(MATTHEW 16:24-25)

Donkeys grazing on private property near Callaway Gardens, Georgia, March 24, 2013

Donkeys were made with a cross pattern on their backs, and humbly carry the burdens of others. They are a reminder of Jesus who rode on a donkey's colt into Jerusalem and humbly bore our sins in His death on a cross. Like Jesus, donkeys deny themselves to please their master. Jesus always pleased His Father. *"Jesus said to them … I do nothing on my own authority, but speak just as the Father taught me. And he who sent me is with me. He has not left me alone, for I always do the things that are pleasing to him.'"* (John 8:28-29). In Jesus we too can submit all to God and do the things that please Him.

"Seek the LORD while he may be found; call upon him while he is near; let the wicked forsake his way, and the unrighteous man his thoughts; let him return to the LORD, that he may have compassion on him, and to our God, for he will abundantly pardon." (ISAIAH 55:6-7)

Beartooth mountains, Wyoming, August 17, 2010

Jackson Lake, Wyoming, August 7, 2007

The righteous God hates sin and warns people to forsake their wicked ways. God caused bears to attack people who challenged the credibility of the prophet Elisha. Some small boys *"jeered at him ... And two she-bears came out of the woods and tore forty-two of the boys"* (2 Kings 2:23a-24). In Jesus strength, love God and turn from unrighteous thoughts and ways. God will abundantly pardon the sins of those who seek Him.

"As a deer pants for flowing streams, so pants my soul for you, O God. My soul thirsts for God, for the living God. When shall I come and appear before God?" (PSALM 42:1-2)

Leigh Lake Trail, Teton National Park, August 14, 2016

Knowing God in His might, mercy, goodness and sovereignty, we thirst for Him. We seek to submit to Him today and in the future. We will fully be with God in the new earth in our resurrected bodies. "*And I heard a loud voice from the throne saying, 'Behold, the dwelling place of God is with man. He will dwell with them, and they will be his people, and God himself will be with them as their God'*" (Revelation 21:3).

"Fear the Lord and serve Him and obey His voice and not rebel"

The book of Samuel helps us to see the godly examples of Hannah and her son, Samuel, and David. They submitted to God and were blessed.

Hannah prayed to God as the LORD of Hosts (all created agencies and forces) and poured out her soul before Him (1 Samuel 1:15).

Samuel responded to the LORD's call saying, *"Speak, for your servant hears"* (1 Samuel 3:10). When Samuel was old, he addressed the people with God's wisdom:

> "If you will fear the LORD and serve him and obey his voice and not rebel against the commandment of the LORD, and if both you and the king who reigns over you will follow the LORD your God, it will be well. But if you will not obey the voice of the LORD, but rebel against the commandment of the LORD, then the hand of the LORD will be against you and your king."
>
> (1 SAMUEL 12:14-15)

King Saul sought his own ways. His jealousy and anger over David's favor with God caused Saul to fall deeper and deeper into sin.

Air pollution from the fire in Blackforest, Colorado, which destroyed 509 homes, and caused 38,000 people to evacuate, June 2012

"For if we go on sinning deliberately after receiving the knowledge of the truth, there no longer remains a sacrifice for sins, but a fearful expectation of judgment, and a fury of fire that will consume the adversaries." (HEBREWS 10:26-27)

"Therefore let us be grateful for receiving a kingdom that cannot be shaken, and thus let us offer to God acceptable worship, with reverence and awe, for our God is a consuming fire."

(HEBREWS 12:28-29)

"And without faith it is impossible to please him, for whoever would draw near to God must believe that he exists and that he rewards those who seek him." (HEBREWS 11:6)

"General" as a Kitten, Elizabeth, Colorado, September 29, 2012

The kitten, pictured here 6 years ago, has become a treasure to my wife (see page 77). Lida is so touched when the seemingly self-reliant creature is excited by her presence and decides to run to her to receive her love and care. There is a special understanding between them that speaks of the goodness of God who satisfies us with gladness. Sometimes we are like the cat in exhibiting self-reliance, yet still conscious that we are dependent on God. In faith, we turn to our Maker and know that we will receive His steadfast love.

"'God opposes the proud, but gives grace to the humble.' Submit yourselves therefore to God." (JAMES 4:6-7)

Honeybee seeks pollen from Choke Cherry blossoms, Elizabeth, Colorado, May 12, 2018

Honeybees follow God's purpose by giving their lives in service. A drone does not have a stinger, has large eyes to find the queen and dies after mating with her. The male drones are typically dragged out of the hive without resistance by the females in the fall to die in the cold, apparently to conserve honey. Females also die in service by stinging any threats to the hive. The bees bless us by pollinating plants and making honey. They help us to know that fruits result from a life of humble submission to God that go beyond the servant's comprehension. Praise God that this behavior is possible for us in Christ.

"Be still before the Lord and wait patiently for him." (PSALM 37:7A)

Blue Heron, Crested Butte, Colorado, July 12, 2018

The great blue heron matches the color of the rocks along the bank. The reflection in the water shows that the bird is standing on one leg. The crooks in the branches are like the crooks in the bird's neck. It is a picture of peace. There is so much to notice—God sees it all and loves it because it glorifies Him. The heron is patient and is rewarded with life. *"For God Alone, O my soul, wait in silence, for my hope is from him ... On God rests my salvation and my glory; my mighty rock, my refuge is God"* (Psalm 62:5,7).

"Rejoice always, pray without ceasing, give thanks in all circumstances; for this is the will of God in Christ Jesus for you."
(1 THESSALONIANS 5:17-18)

Praying Mantis, Elizabeth, Colorado, October, 1, 2018

I disturbed this praying mantis so that it moved. Typically, a praying mantis is in a prayer position as it waits camouflaged in the grass for a meal.

When your children see this creature in all excitement, tell them that the insect can remind us to pray continuously as we wait on the Lord.

Answers to prayer are typically beyond what we imagine.

"Now to Him who is able to do exceedingly abundantly above all that we ask or think, according to the power that works in us, to Him be glory in the church by Christ Jesus to all generations, forever and ever. Amen" (Ephesians 3:20-21).

"Oh give thanks to the LORD, for he is good, for his steadfast loves endures forever! Let them thank the LORD for his steadfast love, for his wondrous works to the children of man! For he satisfies the longing soul, and the hungry soul he fills with good things." (PSALM 107:1, 8-9)

Barn Swallows chicks receiving good food by air delivery, Elizabeth, Colorado, July 2, 2016

Apart from Jesus, we are as helpless as baby birds. *"Whoever abides in me and I in him, he it is that bears much fruit, for apart from me you can do nothing"* (John 15:5). Giving ourselves to God involves a longing for His actions in our lives. We wait on Him, depend on His provision and expect His steadfast love. As we walk with Him we see that He is faithful and gives all that we need to serve Him. He is trustworthy. *"Wait for the LORD; be strong, and let your heart take courage; wait for the LORD!"* (Psalm 27:14). *"His divine power has granted to us all things that pertain to life and godliness, through the knowledge of him who called us to his own glory and excellence"* (2 Peter 1:3). What can be more satisfying than God's steadfast love and a life that gives God glory?

"Four things on earth are small, but they are exceedingly wise: the ants are a people not strong, yet they provide their food in the summer; the rock badgers are a people not mighty, yet they make their homes in the cliffs; the locusts have no king, yet all of them march in rank; the lizard you can take in your hands, yet it is in kings' palaces." (PROVERBS 30:24-28)

Yellow-Bellied Marmot, Aspen, Colorado, July 12, 2018

A marmot, like a rock badger, is wise to live among the protection of rocks. They are a living parable teaching us to live in the shelter of God through Jesus our Savior. *"God is our refuge and strength, a very present help in trouble"* (Psalm 46:1). In our own power, we fail to resist the temptations of the world to selfish living. But praise be to God for Jesus Christ in us and the workings of the Holy Spirit, who give us strength to live holy lives for God. Christ works through His body, the church, to encourage us to be alive to God in unity, like locusts who march in rank. *"And let us consider how to stir up one another to love and good works, not neglecting to meet together, as is the habit of some, but encouraging one another, and all the more as you see the Day drawing near"* (Hebrews 10:24-25).

"But none says, 'Where is God my Maker, who gives songs in the night, who teaches us more than the beasts of the earth and makes us wiser than the birds of the heavens?'" (JOB 35:10-11)

Great Horned owl, Elizabeth, Colorado, August 24, 2018

Owls hoot in the night and are made to fly without making a sound. They are a common symbol of wisdom. In Christ, He makes us wiser than the owl. Let God's creation impress upon us that He is worth seeking. Pursue our God and Maker, the source of wisdom. *"If any of you lacks wisdom, let him ask God … in faith"* (James 1:5-6). *"The beginning of wisdom is this: Get wisdom, and whatever you get, get insight. Prize her highly, and she will exalt you"* (Proverbs 4:7-8a). *"Be not wise in your own eyes; fear the Lord, and turn away from evil"* (Proverbs 3:7).

"Commit your work to the LORD, and your plans will be established."

(PROVERBS 16:3)

Elizabeth, Colorado, February 13, 2011

Canada geese, Elizabeth, Colorado, November 8, 2014

It is refreshing to hear flocks of geese flying overhead because they remind us that the living God establishes our paths. The geese praise God with their particular honking sounds as they move on the straight way God provides.

The examples of God's absolute guidance of migrating birds assures us that God will bless our steps as we delight in His Word. Submit to God.

"Trust in the Lord with all your heart, and do not lean on your own understanding. In all your ways acknowledge him, and he will make straight your paths." (Proverbs 3:5-6)

"So then let us pursue what makes for peace and for mutual up building."
(ROMANS 14:19)

Canada Geese, Elizabeth, Colorado, February 19, 2018

Canada geese gracefully settle in on a frosty February day in the stubble of a Colorado wheatfield. God's creatures and scattered frost illustrate a picture of the peace of God. He makes peace in our life! It is something to seek from God as a fruit of the spirit. *"But the fruit of the Spirit is love, joy, peace, patience, kindness, goodness, faithfulness, gentleness, self-control; against such things there is no law"* (Galatians 5:22-23). When we submit to God and let Him know our requests, we can experience His peace. *"Do not be anxious about anything, but in everything by prayer and supplication with thanksgiving let your requests be made known to God. And the peace of God, which surpasses all understanding, will guard your hearts and your minds in Christ Jesus"* (Philippians 4:6-7).

"Praise the LORD … he makes peace in your borders: he fills you with the finest of the wheat … he scatters frost like ashes" (Psalm 147:12, 14, 16).

"The wolf shall dwell with the lamb, and the leopard shall lie down with the young goat, and the calf and the lion and the fattened calf together; and a little child shall lead them. The cow and the bear shall graze; their young shall lie down together; and the lion shall eat straw like the ox. The nursing child shall play over the hole of the cobra, and the waned child shall put his hand on the adder's den. They shall not hurt or destroy in all my holy mountain; for the earth shall be full of the knowledge of the LORD as the waters cover the sea." (ISAIAH 11:6-9)

Black leopard, Wildlife World, Litchfield Park, Arizona, December 28, 2013

Calf, Elizabeth, Colorado, April 29, 2014

The world's way is to suppress the truth. We need to stop conforming to the world and proclaim the truth. Be bold and confident that some day all will know God. Remarkably, in that time, God will cause humans and animals to live in harmony. There is a connection between our relationship with God and the redemption of creatures. Submit to the mission of King Jesus as He redeems the world.

Pronghorn among the sage, Casper, Wyoming, August 8, 2010

"Fear not, you beasts of the field, for the pastures of the wilderness are green." (JOEL 2:22)

Bison Bull in Lamar Valley has a deep voice that seemingly moans for green pastures. Wyoming, July 29, 2018

The land and the beasts on it all suffer in the hands of people who do not acknowledge God. *"For the evil of those who dwell in it [land] the beasts and the birds are swept away"* (Jeremiah 12:4a). But God is merciful. If people will return to Him with all their heart, with fasting and weeping, he will be gracious. He will no longer make His people a reproach among the nation and the beasts of the field will be blessed with green pastures.

"Now may the God of hope fill you with all joy and peace in believing"
(ROMANS 15:13A)

The core problem in the world today is a low view of God (Synder, 2016). This perspective corresponds with a high view of self. As a consequence, Christ's work on the cross is not properly received with thanksgiving and renewed hearts of righteousness. The external crises of the day (e.g., marriage, health, environment) come from walking as slaves to sin. There is a sin crisis at the core (Brown, 2018). This is why science, education and politics tend to fall short of meeting the goals—they do not address the core issue. The solution to sin is Jesus. The church needs to pray for the Holy Spirit to regenerate the hearts of people and nations. Those who walk with the Creator-Jesus will take care of His creation motivated by love for the Savior-Jesus and His Word. The love multiplies as the care of plants and creatures increase the "CreationSpeech" about the truths of Scripture. The cycle of encouragement to righteousness is the process of sanctification.

"Blessed is the man who walks not in the counsel of the wicked, nor stands in the way of sinners, nor sits in the seat of scoffers; but his delight is in the law of the Lord, and on his law he meditates day and night."
(PSALM 1:1-2)

"I am speaking in human terms, because of your natural limitations. For just as you once presented your members as slaves to impurity and to lawlessness leading to more lawlessness, so now present your members as slaves to righteousness leading to sanctification."
(ROMANS 6:19)

I was privileged to see this Desert Tortoise and learn that it was made to live where there is little water, intense heat, and few predators or fires.

"And God said, 'Let the earth bring forth ... creeping things ... according to their kinds.' And it was so." (GENESIS 1:24)

Young tortoises survive best where they are camouflaged among rocks and can find native plants for burrow cover and food. However, inconsiderate actions threaten desert ecosystems. Introducing invasive plants fuel fires that kill turtles. Exposed trash, road kill and water enable ravens to thrive. Ravens peck through the top of the soft shells of the young eliminating half of them. Tortoise shells harden after 6 years, freeing the reptiles to dig burrows for multiple inhabitants, distribute seeds of native plants, and fascinate man with God's goodness.

Consider the metaphor. When man is governed by God's word, the people prosper (Psalm 1). As sinful man removed the armor of God from the culture, children were bombarded by destructive lies and worthless idols. The few that put on the truth have liberty to serve the reigning Lord Jesus and live out their purpose to give glory to God. As it will take a long time to restore desert habitats after they have been disturbed, it will take time to restore humanist societies to live by the Word of God. Let each of us do what God has called us to do in Jesus.

Pray and wait with hope. Expect to be amazed.

Mojave Desert, Nevada, October 22, 2018

"Only fear the Lord and serve Him faithfully with all your heart."
(1 Samuel 12:24)

"Behold, with the clouds of heaven there came one like a son of man …
And to him was given dominion and glory and a kingdom,
that all peoples, nations, and languages should serve him."
(DANIEL 7:13-14)

Mule deer bucks at sunset, Parker, Colorado, October 3, 2014

"I have no greater joy than to hear that my children are walking in the truth." (3 JOHN 1:4)

I hope this book helps you to know that God's creation can help the next generation to see God, like it helped Job (page 10). Creation testifies to the truth of God's Word. In believing the truth, God fills one with joy and peace. So I encourage you to observe God's creatures with your families to increase their faith and joy. Consider some of the outdoor activities that were helpful to me.

- Raise and care for fish, puppies, kittens, chickens, bees. Go to a zoo, aquarium
- Establish nature sanctuaries (meadow, prairie, wildflower garden, stand of trees)
- Drive in the country and keep a camera handy to capture observations
- Hike, float, fish in wilderness areas, conservation areas, National Parks
- Participate or attend reenactments, homesteading events, historical villages

As more and more knowledge of the truth is accepted in the Spirit, and as one dies more to self, one can experience increasing joy and peace and hope, encouraging more learning. This is the process of sanctification. "Sanctify them in the truth: your word is truth" (John 17:17).

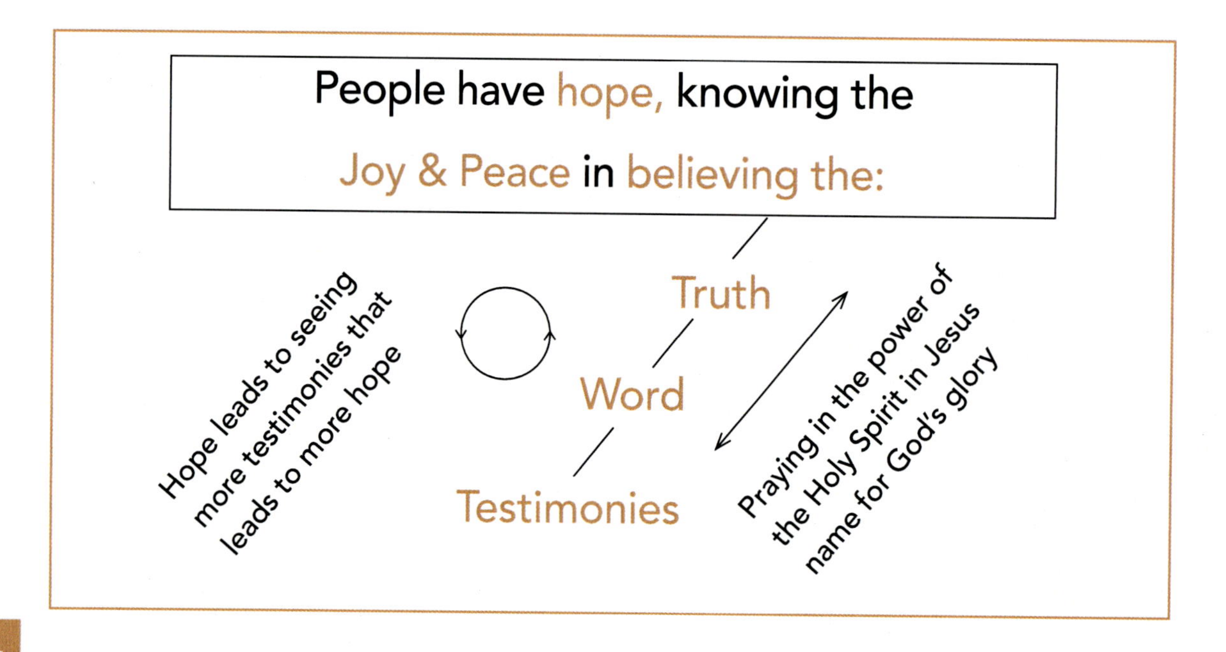

"On the glorious splendor of your majesty, and on your wondrous works, I will meditate." (PSALM 145:5)

Observe beetles, beans, birds, flowers, puppies, rocks, streams, sunsets, leafs, berries etc. Take notes, photographs, make sketches.

Ask:

- What do we know about it? What is its name? Seek interesting facts
- Is it mentioned in Scripture?
- Does it help us understand a verse in Scripture?
- Could its nature or behavior be a metaphor of wisdom in the Word?
- Has anyone else gained Scriptural insights from it?
- Does the timing and experience of seeing it reveal the providence and sovereignty of God?
- Is it for my encouragement; to share with others; for a specific person in need?
- What attributes and interrelationships enable it to be here so many years after the time of creation and the worldwide flood?
- How can we help it to thrive for the Holy Spirit to use in future generations for God's glory?

"They shall speak of the might of your awesome deeds, and I will declare your greatness" (PSALM 145:6)

The Psalm continues to describe God's greatness as: might, goodness, righteousness, steadfast love, mercy, power, dominion, kindness, nearness, protection. (Psalm 145:7-20)

REFERENCES

Bao W, Rong Y, Rong S, Liu L. 2012. Dietary iron intake, body iron stores, and the risk of type 2 diabetes: a systematic review and meta-analysis. BMC Med. 10:119-132.

Blumberg, WE, Peisach, J. 1965. An electron spin resonance study of copper uroporphyrin III and other touraco feather components. J. Biol. Chem. 240:870-876.

Brown, Edward. 2018. *Our Father's World: Mobilizing the Church to Care for Creation.* Intervarsity Press., Downers Grove, IL.

Cross AJ, Harnly JM, Ferrucci LM, Risch A, Mayne ST, Sinha R. 2012. Developing a heme iron database for meats according to meat type, cooking method and doneness level. Food Nutr Sci. 3:905-913.

Fonseca-Nunes A, Jakszyn P, Agudo A. 2014. Iron and cancer risk--a systematic review and meta-analysis of the epidemiological evidence. Cancer Epidemiol Biomarkers Prev. 23:12-31.

Hochgraf, JS, Waters JS, Socha JJ. 2018. Patterns of Tracheal Compression in the Thorax of the Ground Beetle, Platynus decentis. Yale J Biol Med. 91:409-430

Hunnicutt J, He K, Xun P, 2014. Dietary iron intake and body iron stores are associated with risk of coronary heart disease in a meta-analysis of prospective cohort studies. J Nutr.:144:359-366.

Magnino, S, Colin P, Dei-Cas E et al. 2009. Biological risks associated with consumption of reptile products. Int J Food Microbial 134:163-175.

Rushdoony, R.J. 1973. *Institutes of Biblical Law, Vol. 1*, (Phillipsburg, NJ: Presbyterian and Reformed Publishing), pp.. Pages 301-302.

Synder, J. 2016. *Behold Your God: Rethinking God Biblically - Daily Devotional Workbook.* Media Gratiae (Christ Church Media, Inc.), New Albany, Mississippi.

Walter, JS, 2013. Dynamics of tracheal compression in the horned passalus beetle. Am J Physiol Regul Integr Comp Physiol. 304:R621-627

INDEX OF ANIMALS

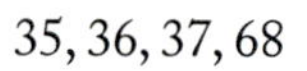

Peacock train feathers (could be used to consider the glory of the the train of the Lord's robe as He sits on the throne, Isaiah 6:1), Denver Zoo, Colorado, March 18, 2019